TRÁITHNÍNÍ

Lis,
John
ottawa 2000

JOHN ENNIS

DEDALUS

Dublin 2000

The Dedalus Press
24 The Heath ~ Cypress Downs ~ Dublin 6W
Ireland

Cover design by Simon Webb
[a young designer working in Waterford Institute of Technology.
He believes that one day he will change the world]

ISBN 1 901233 53 7 (paper)
ISBN 1 901233 54 5 (bound)

[John Ennis is Head of Humanities at Waterford Institute of
Technology. His "Selected Poems" were published in1996
' by The Dedalus Press]

Dedalus Press books are represented and distributed in the U.S.A.
and Canada by **Dufour Editions Ltd.**, P.O. Box 7, Chester
Springs, Pennsylvania 19425
in the UK by **Central Books**, 99 Wallis Road, London E9 5LN

The Dedalus Press receives financial assistance from
An Chomhairle Ealaíon, The Arts Council, Ireland.
Printed in Dublin by Colour Books Ltd

TRÁITHNÍNÍ

Tráithnín : *a dart or arrow, a strong blade of grass, a withered stalk of meadow grass, a thraneen or blade of grass etc* (Irish-English Dictionary, Patrick S. Dinneen M.A.) *Dry grass-stalk. "Leagfá le tráithnín mé"* : *"you could have knocked me down with a feather"* (Niall O'Donaill's Dictionary)

for
Jean Bizimana,
going home to Burundi

1

Here comes
the meadower
he plucks
a tall stalk

sips the stem
while the field
screams,
calls to its sister.

A tremor
amid the swathes,
heads nod
in a crowd.

The meadower
walks all over us.

2

The meadower
little macho
man all machine

the things
he's said
and done

written on
kingdom come
and beyond:

his mate's
good as he is
cutting swathes

through our souls.
Those ghouls.

3

Constellations
shone
for me
once.

You've taken
the sun
the stars
the moon

from me,
left me
a dry stalk.

Yet see the wind
tongue
my lips.

4

Brother sedge
sister rush
down there in
the hollow

the cutter
may yet skirt you.
Remember us
in the calm twilight.

You are only
a corner swathe or so
away from where
our calligraphy

came to
grief.

5

Field mouse,
your timid
snout moves
amid stems,

dutch and rye
timothy,
these homes
from home;

nose round
these poems.

On this stalk
a ladybird
hangs on
my every word.

6

That game
we played
as children.

We'd set
tráithníní
crossways
in the jaw.

Between the teeth
of the unsuspecting.
Yanked stems.

Left the other
to spit out
a mouthful
of seed.

7

I will make
of you and Me
this meadow
God said.

Here
we go,
steppes
prairies

to feast
the eye.
Mates for
the soul

modelled
from soil.

8

I am
the hare
who once
hid in your form

in the curled fragrance
of your spikelets
even if you wilt
to a field of falling stems.

Once for love
I made a whorl
of the rye grass
in your house,

Forgive me
for this.

9

My friend, the rye
germinating early
what's your hurry.

Give us time,
time to pause
space to consider
your gullible leaves.

There will be plenty
(plenty to ponder on)
seeking shelter
in collapsing swathes.

Foragers.
Ourselves
like cringing
animals.

10

I sowed trees
in the meadow
so the mowers
couldn't enter.

Said I'd raise
wild flowers
with timothy.

Today, sycamore
elm, poplar
damson

are outed
abandon
my willow field
to the machine.

11

The blade

is in
your swathe
my friend
these days

these heady
days
that know
no end.

O watch
your front
your back,

the edge
is close.

12

Once you
called my
name.
I was

alive.
That day
twelve months
ago.

A long
time to
wait in
the stalk

for you,
my love.

13

We stretched out
together
where the grass
grew high

my arm
across you
our faces
close,

your nipple
rose like
a cenotaph

where
no flowers
lay.

14

I've seen
the last
entrance
of your face;

like velvet
these panicles,
our dreams
the same,

like swathes
falling
round me
the hours
the days.

Exit.

15

The hail sky's
hate white
ice
floes.

What people
are these
falling
swathewise?

Pentecost
shines
with frost.

No
mowing
yet.

16

As we grew tall
you took Frost's road
on the tar to Darwin,
our air was nearly

as we know it
if deteriorating.
But not as ozone
less as tomorrow.

You have cut
swathes around us
mastered the dawn
and then full noon

left us to exhale on your sad victories
past midnight and the fall moon.

17

i.m. W.Owen

Fellow stalker,
I want
to lie down
with you.

Our stems
can't stem
this war's
red sap.

Soon we
will have
our way.

Pull closer.
The blade
approaches.

18

i.m. F.Ledwidge

'And hide
your face
against
my name',
like your meadows
to flow over
the rims.

Round Slane
to know mauve
in the throat only, love
salt drop

in the sea
of drought
and tears.

19

Mecca within reach
entering Jerusalem
or the warm Ganges

we hosanna
into the blades.
Assailing
the hedges

of our dreams
day after day
we still stand
rooted, if blind,
in the old fixations.

Siva's pilgrims
for all that.

20

Dew on us
in early dawn
late evening

those times
vulnerable
as swathes

hope we stand
here we fall
on your streets

waiting for
the rains
to show

pity
on us.

21

I remember
Cui Jian, guitarist
a young singer
trumpet player

in Tienanmen,
leading vocalist
in a group, crying

'I feel blood
flows through you
because you have
a hand that's warm'.

Stood tall and proud
was brought to earth
in that field of millions ...

22

... 'I cannot walk
nor can I weep,
my body is
getting dry,
I want to stay
always with you..

Your hand is firmly
held in mine.
You are
not made of iron
though you are just
as strong a form.

I feel like drinking water.
You stop me speaking with your mouth ...

23

I say I want
to go with you,
your hand is
holding mine.

I feel this is
no desert here
can't see the soil's
cracked with drought.

The day you used
a piece of red cloth
to cover my eyes
and the sky above us

you asked me what I saw.
I said that I saw happiness.'

24

We have seen
wind and rain
wrestle
other fields

and thought
of them:
today
it's our turn

to sink
in the deluge
of the quotidian.
Flat out.

Sideways in the sun
come back to our standing.

25

When will
we see
the end
of storms
glittering pools
in meadows,
forecasts
of more?

We are
the field
you saw
cut down
weeks ago
sodden, unmade.

26

Or we grew up
in an ugly time
for the stem

sap in the prepuce
before our prime,
so much herbage,
the seeping verbiage

of the silage fathers.
We were cut
in suicidal fields.
We were gathered

into stinking plastic
with white crosses
to scare crows.

27

We have fallen
with the swathe
of despond
no one

to touch us
these long weeks
of gales
and rain;

bronzed,
a pallor
took us over
then the grey,

blackness
on our lips.

28

While you wept
dividing my ties
I was writing
of meadows.

When you drove off the children
I was writing of Timothy.

When you stripped tiles
over my head
I was tethering rows.

When you spoke my name
I gazed over swathes.

When you left
I flourished in
the mountain field.

29

I say
I am
all right
what's the point

whispering
otherwise?
The sap
is disappearing

in the stem.
We're fodder
for sharpening
histories.

You would frighten
like a quail if I told you.

30

Panicles blow
in the wind
to and fro
like we can't

as the wren
lights on stems
sips their seed
in pollinate

glory. We're
trapped
along the mearin
crabbed

hesitant
non-communicant.

31

Lie down
in the grass
the sharp edge intimates,
know each stalk
root to rachis.

Each blade
is novel
with no finale.

If we
have not even seen
this field's beginning,

how can we
comprehend
its end?

32

Pollen rides the wind
grace to the heart,
so many stems alive.
Yes, you could sail

the seas with Timothy
rye and Dutch
all the swathes

like traffic lanes
to and fro and
over and back
multitudinous

and never so
beautiful as in
their last days.

33

The scent
of the 29th
where we lay.
We had it made.

Absence, like a blade,
shines in the dew.
Your heart is breaking.
I turn

over a withering swathe.
Inhaling
the making
of June,

I   think
of you.

34

You sip
the stem
that's me,
my love.

This sap
like none
before.

It was
so in
Eden
once

millennia
ago,
my love.

35

We breathe in
the vetches
where new seed
overhangs
the aged.

We have stretched
full length
in the grasses
seen the clouds
in the gale

skimming the blue
sail another sea.

You come
with me.

36

Come back
to this sun:
I'll make
room

for stalk
blooms
beyond all
recall

speech
finger
and
touch

in this meadow,
lie lengthwise.

37

We'd tender
the sweet stalk
of Timothy
in our fingers

hours before
the dews
wet them,
sun set

get up
walk off.
Love was
a swathe

care free
field free.

38

The sky
is blue

above us,
what is
there to fear,
we're stalk

to stalk
as the wind
above our heads

exhales over
in the sycamore,

moves us
side by side
in a clover bed.

39

Machinery
at the gap
has not mown
yet into us.

For an hour
pollen waves
a full tide heaves,
grass.

So many
shades of mauve
that never neap,
ebb.

Eternal
midsummer.

40

I grow
within these walls
in their prime
in their ruin.

My stalk
muscles
so far up

I give and take
all life
in me

through days
that shake
the seed
from me.

41

Featherheads
reach
with copious seed
up toward the moon

gleam. The sun
warms
our poignant mauves
in every breeze:

as one stalk leans
against another twinned
entwined

just so
in the wind
are we.

42

I live
the tenderness
of seed grass.
I salve
dumbheads
feel the blade
write a hymn
out of them.

My thighs
warm
your byres.

I love Timothy,
rye grass too
and esparto.

43

Sweet stalk, let us be.
In our gazing, let us be

as vigorous
as the wind
across grassy
continents.

My seed
spurt and sprout about me.
Winter
without me.

Son,
your business is ovens.
Gristle to the plates
of the unwary.

44

We are
not wheat
are men
of lesser

protein
feed
for cattle
that graze

breadward
in this vale
of fallen
soulmaking.

Nothing so becomes us
as our leaving.

45

The full beasts
in us move on

house us in fields
for copulation

birth, re-insemination.
If they looked once

to our condition
in their eyes

in their cud
they would savour

our spendthrift seed
here in Belsen,

the cries of children
outside the ovens.

46

So, are you up
for cutting too?
Your loins
to collapse
on clay?
Your golden anthers
to loosen?

Take a breather
of white stigma
the silken tips
of any prairie,
meadower,

where meadows start
at your name.

47

Says
the seed head
nodding to
itself —

poor eunuch
over the erection
it fought for:
'I want to die,

I've shot
my bolt. This dawn I was.
This dark I am
not'.

Rise, child, save your face.
Fodder the cliché.

48

I want to bow
out in the legume
break like a stalk
when the vellum

lows to its calf
and the last milk
is suckled dry
in white sap:

in the spirit
of an October sun-shower
as after love, a sudden
gust.

Yes. One good clean
snap in the wind.

49

Let us have
our autumn
and our winter.
Don't rush us
into spring.

We enter
our companions.

We poor
beasts loom
on shorn
meadows.

The rainy
heavens
abandon us.

50

Give us
an embrace
of stars
after the dark
daylight.

Give us
cattle stir
fox covert
rabbit sleep

frogleap
fieldmouse
at our feet,

the last
landrail.

51

Dew in their nodding
grown heavy
with talk
and affection,

like a swathe
the uncles fall
in the one space
handful of days.

Pensioner Solomons.
'Look how we slaved!
Look how we toiled
down another's field!'

Like old bible lilies
on their last pins.

52

One day
I pierced
the clay.
Light hurt.

I embraced
my scream.
The dew dried
on me.

My red
mother
healed.
I nod

down today to
her.

53

Teens, early manhood
the faces of
my seven brothers
pose about me
[shortest stalk

in their midst]
as the old photo
records, our father
in his braces

with our mother,
the nectar-rich
white bloom
of bindweed
in her hand.

54

I shudder
in the stem
when I remember
how their breath caught:

she, his teenage bride
come to his deathbed.
I saw them engaged
in a hospital ward:

their eyes meeting as
in their early days
making love by the fields
before the children came.

Now their lives are rent,
a living sacrament.

55

They would not
crush the meadows
with their love

so, between twin banks
where the primroses
came in hundreds

along the mountain
field headland in
a cart-way dip

with white limbs
tenderness to spare
they entered as one

afternoons
in the sun.

56

They fell
in fullness
in their
eighties

tall stalks
on their side
their thighs adrift
after nine children.

Breathing their last
I was in their field.
They died in leaf
and in full seed.

Their meadows live on
in me.

57

Above us
the stars slip
from the sky
like fathers

and mothers
sisters, brothers
from the chairs
by their fires

that warmed us
once as visitors.
Where are we,

in what swathe,
when Venus
fades at dawn?

58

A little bother,
brother,
knocks you over
rocks you now

side to side.
Years ago well-rooted
in storms,
you secured abandoned

coulter anchors
across outhouses
what might be
blown

      cocks
          ricks

59

The old meadows
drift away like mirages,

but, often, I saw my father
gather a field up in his arms

in the heat of the sun
and the blue zenith of noon

inhale the aroma of hay
        like a fine scent
read the fallen swathes
        like a testament

as we leant on our forks
amid the windrows
waiting for the word,
the field to be saved.

60

Waiting for
us to fall
shed seed
in sunlight:

daughters, sons
springing to
fullness,sap
in full bloom.

We nod
towards the gap.
Flesh and blood
grow up round us.

Far summers.
Make room.

61

How the grasses
ache
to be
other

than the frail
frail stalks
they are

gesticulating
in the wind
to the end

deflowered
on the earth
dependable,
expendable.

62

In that last swathe
I was loath
falling.
Why linger on?

The sun shone
bright as your face
in that hour.
Thousands

stood round me.
Now there's only
threats
of storm,

fork lightning
on the horizon.

63

Your secrets
fond scents
die
with you.

This swathe
is maybe not
our last one.
Bring it down

round the field
before you
go. Back swathe.
It's worth a cut.

See it fall
to complete mortality.

64

Good people,
men, women
going to seed
you see them

on corridors
acrid with wars
sour haze
not pollen,

will none
swathe
their talents
in a meadow

full of aroma,
love?

65

This is winter.
I know it
in the absence
of caresses

of a breeze
touching stems,
Timothy and rye.
All my familiars

in fullness once,
real opulence.
This is winter
not to walk

the high
grasses.

66

They should
have been
long shorn,
these fields.

In their prime.
Not forgotten
till the hoar
frosts of autumn.

We are, my loves,
talking ourselves
toward the snow
the broken blades

in a field
no one cut.

67

Yes. To
go whole, able
bodied in the blessed
fragrance,

that would have once been
tolerable.

Sun
to swathe
our last
days.

Only we
dance in
the breeze
remaining.

68

Some need
the bole
the trunk
strength.

It's as if
these male
uprights
survive.

Role models!
These days
I gloss
meadows.

My vision's
a tráithnín.

69

I am cut
adrift, my sole function
is to seed you.
I am then

redundant.
We make gods
out of mortals
go through the stalkjerks

of affection.
In our embrace
the heart lays bare
the shorn places.

We slip towards the blade. Wait,
Our juicy souls were made for it.

70

I knew
this hour
would come
when I'd

be cut off
from myself
dew cooling
my warmth

day
over
and
done

only to wait
for the gathering.

71

What leaves
you so sure
this stem's
sturdier

come fall?

Why do
you raise
my hopes
in vain?

You walk
so careless

across
my field
of dreams.

72

What does it profit
to imagine
we could live
nine lives?

Linger like the last
landrails in the grasses
of no
set aside?

Our days come down in
the snide of wind
the belt of rain
just when we thought

these blue forenoons
shone for good.

73

Hawkweed, cinquefoil
buttercup and harebell,
you lean with the meadow vetchling
across the last swathe fall.

Rave at the meadow's cut edge
with the souls of crane's bill
wild fritillaries
in the summer gale

that numbs the rabid tractor's
circling hum.

Hugging the ditch, safe from the blade,
secure in their own cynical glory,
the proud umbels of hogweed
grow old in the shade.

74

We will run
back again
like children
of eight, nine

down your lane
where the swathes
have forgotten us
whose tenants

looked into
the rising sun
one fine dawn
with a mind

to sharpening
sickles for us.

75

To be
severed
when least
expected;

she is gone
he is gone
brought low
in the field:

this is wisdom
to be
cut off
at the root.

Don't expect to see life
in your own lifetime.

76

We felt
his hand
touch us
and so

were driven
profligate
with pollen
for his sandals

the wild
bright gold
of buttercup
for his toes,

gave sap
to his instep.

77

Our falling's
about
to be,
actual.

O no mind
for anything
a blur
of blades

somewhere
to lie
breathe
to the sky.

Infinity
nailed through our palms.

78

Your head
hangs down
one side
your stalk

is broke
the earth's
bereft,
the dead

appear
bleached
swathes.

You reach
out your
arms.

79

The sky
was full
of stars
irrevocable.

A fire
raged in my head
emotion
combustible.

My soul
ran out
the door
after you.

Many meadows
since that time.

80

Cloud shadow
across meadow
we all race

the same road
stalkwise
stalk foolish.

I light candles
at a shrine.

Young then
not yet men
I remember

our laughter
Jimmy Reid
at the mearin.

81

In those teenage years
across plantain-pocked meadows
our loves flushed like red poppies
in no dog-daisy paradise.

Rather, heading rain-flattened
fields, or their rare bronzed companions
we surveyed adolescence
with lovely withering eyes.

The sultry-pressured ceiling above us,
reportage squinting on ditches
we decapped, tidied, remade cocks.

Roughing their clammy butts
we grasped hidden thistles
like first hurts in the fist.

82

We flesh
over the same pastures
again and again
[as if nothing

was ever shorn]
adore the same gods
study old rebuttals
dream new entreaties

steady up the clay
rachis in the wind
opening too for love
spendthrift panicles

long and considered
like Timothy.

83

We hear machinery
work the far corner.
Is it for us too
later on today?

Who will we ask
to walk among us
so that we may

witness to ourselves;
come and then go
toss and waver.

Nothing's fairer
as we stand
like the waves

this blessed day.

84

And just when
we stood
our fairest
the blade

out of nowhere
found
us all
exhalant

without a glint
without flourish
cut us down
at the ankles

our voices falling
side by side in swathes.

85

See us
glide
to the blade
like a fan

a gentle curve
to our falling
dry out
on stubble

to feed
oaken tables
the same faces

the one green faith
in fresh swathes
incarnate.

86

The song birds
have flown
wild plover and all
beating their wings,

we saw them go
[said this is it]
dropping a little
feather or two

voiceless
in flight.
What words
made them so afraid?

That they must quit
their homes with us?

87

With a shuddering
of stem
the blade
passes

this swathe.
To us is born
stalk time
stalk music.

We are
in our prime.

The smell
of sap
is
everywhere.

88

The storms
are over
for now,
like diamonds

the drops
of rain
weight stems
flat, glitter

in sunlight,
we gather
ourselves
together

touch in our limbs
rough as these gems.

89

How wonderful it is
how wonderful
this careful leaning
of stem on stem

no desire to crush
no desire to master
but side by side
in the wavering wind

to know and to hold
our nearness and distance
to give and to take
with support and reason

when dawn opens its arms to noon
and sunset comes with stars.

90

We raise
our heads
towards
the sun,

the dew
slides down
our stems
to the root

in clay.
Breathe out
and touch
the wind.

Enjoy
the earth.

91

Marram
Tramore
I remember
it daily

Fiona
Thérèse
yourself as
in youth

the other three
unborn. Why do

I dream
with closed lids

gull cry
in the sky?

92

After the last
forkfuls
the heaves,
all cocks

conical,
we leave the fields
head
kitchenward

through
the hungry eyes
of the after
grass

like adult
children.

93

Your face on the pillow
and I remembered
a quarter century

of your spine
how love
swerves
in curves,
beauty
flexing
like a bow

my lips
on yours
your lips
on mine.

94

We are
no more
ourselves
save fodder

for our own
to be fed
to uncertain
landscapes

surnames
new vowels
we've become
parents to

hosts
most days.

95

Stalk,
I sip
the juice
the honey bee
passing
sips
from me.

Sap,
we are
born for
you,
our why
in word
and deed.

96

Dispense
your pollen
into the wind
the gales

that blow
from the corner
the breezes
blew gentle

yesterday.
For so it is
gusts
embrace

you in their wake
no more for pity's sake.

97

We ponder
our day
and how
it was

the gulls
kept circling
depressions
passed over

mare's tails
smithy anvils
up in the blue
our only sun

away in the depths
above us.

98

These poems
weak as spindles
knowing nothing
but their falling

a mottled blue,
scented the mind
for a productive
summer season

looked up
for weeks
to grace azure,

this dew-wet
stalk patch
we inhabit.

99

These wisps
of words
I've raked
from air

the furl
blasts
of
everyday.

Other strands
have blown
out of mind.

These settle
as my one
testimony.

100

With this
shuddering
of stem
I thought

I was gone.
Not yet.
Next swathe.
Maybe.

So, let's
luxuriate
a little
in the sun.

Imagining
creation.